SUNSETS and MOONSETS

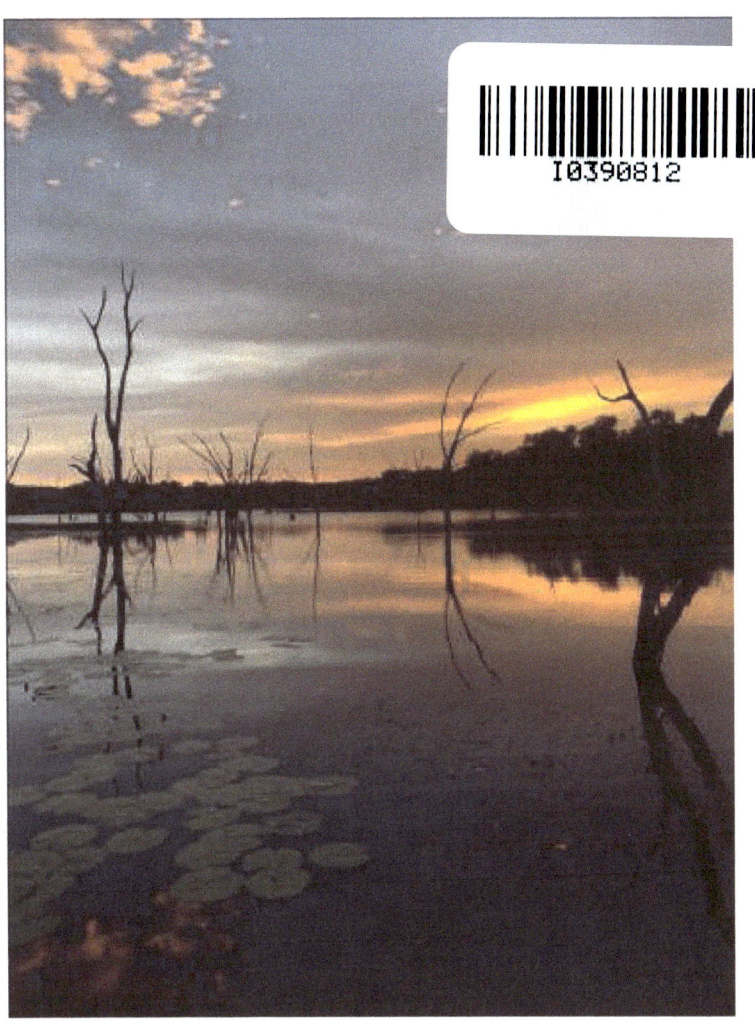

By: *Henry Intili*

Sunsets and Moonsets

Henry Intili

Bainbridge, Georgia 2022

Sunsets and Moonsets is a collection of photos and commentary from our home in Bainbridge, Georgia and from our many travels.

PART 1

SUNSETS

Sunset from our porch in Bainbridge. An August evening in 2021. The pond in the distance (Valentine's Pond) contains the drowned live oaks that died when the pond was formed over 60 years ago. At that time Flint River was dammed to form Seminole Lake, and the local water table rose. The water in three small sink holes poured out forming Valentine's Pond, named after a farmer who lived here many years ago.

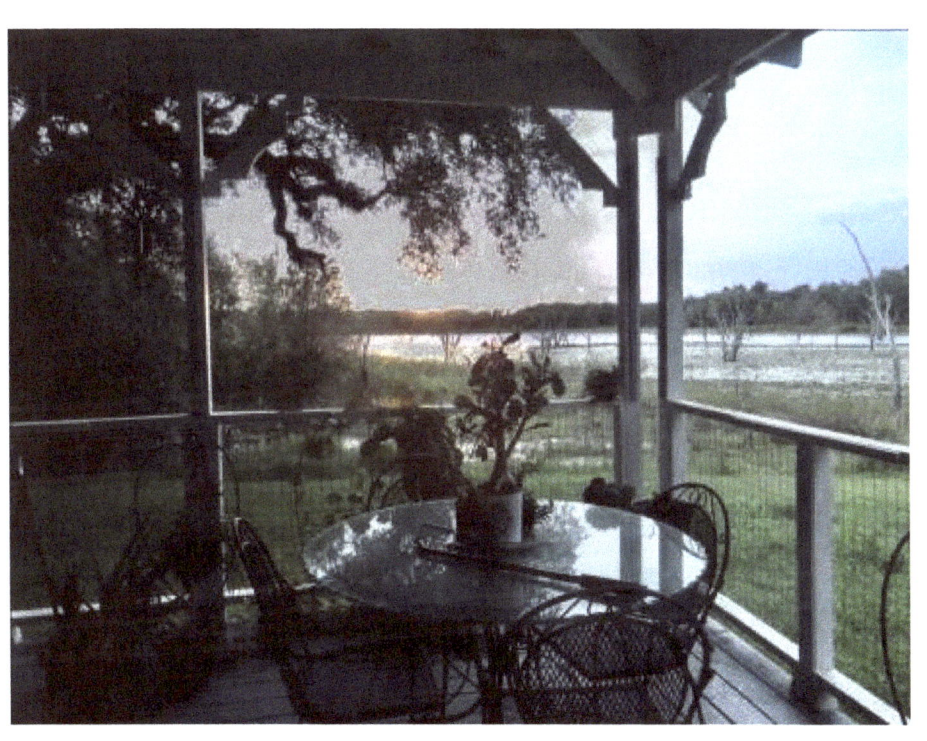

Sunset behind an island in Alaska's Inner Passage gleams off the side of our small cruise ship, The Wilderness Explorer. Early June 2022. The water of the Inner Passage as calm as the sky above.

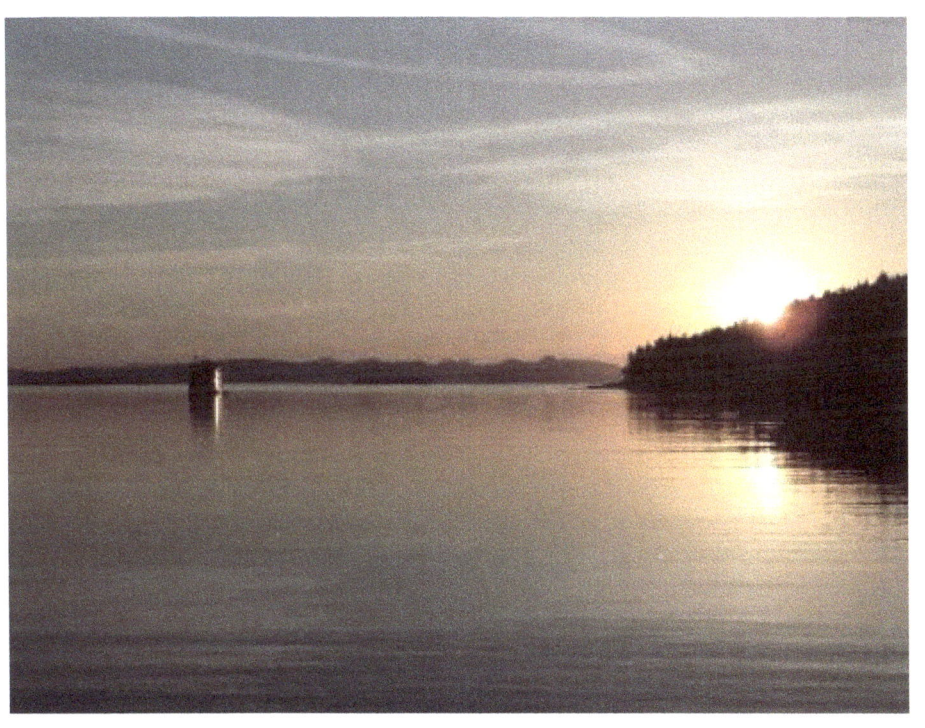

An egret alights on a limb of a drowned live oak in Valentine's Pond during a sunset in May 2019 that bathed everything an eerie red guash.

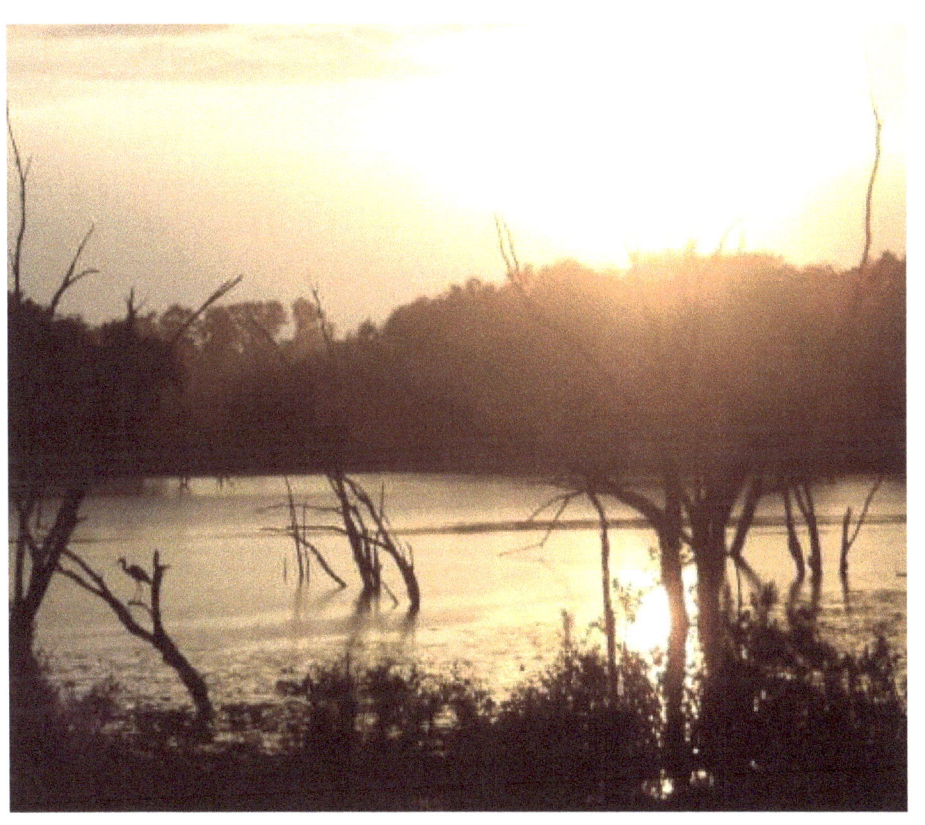

Midnight on the Kokolik River, North Slope, Alaska. This is as close as the sun comes to setting in June above the Arctic Circle. We canoed and explored the treeless tundra for nine days in June 2022. Seemingly empty like the dry grass southern Great Plains, the area contains an abundance of large mammals – caribou, musk ox, grizzly bear, and wolverines.

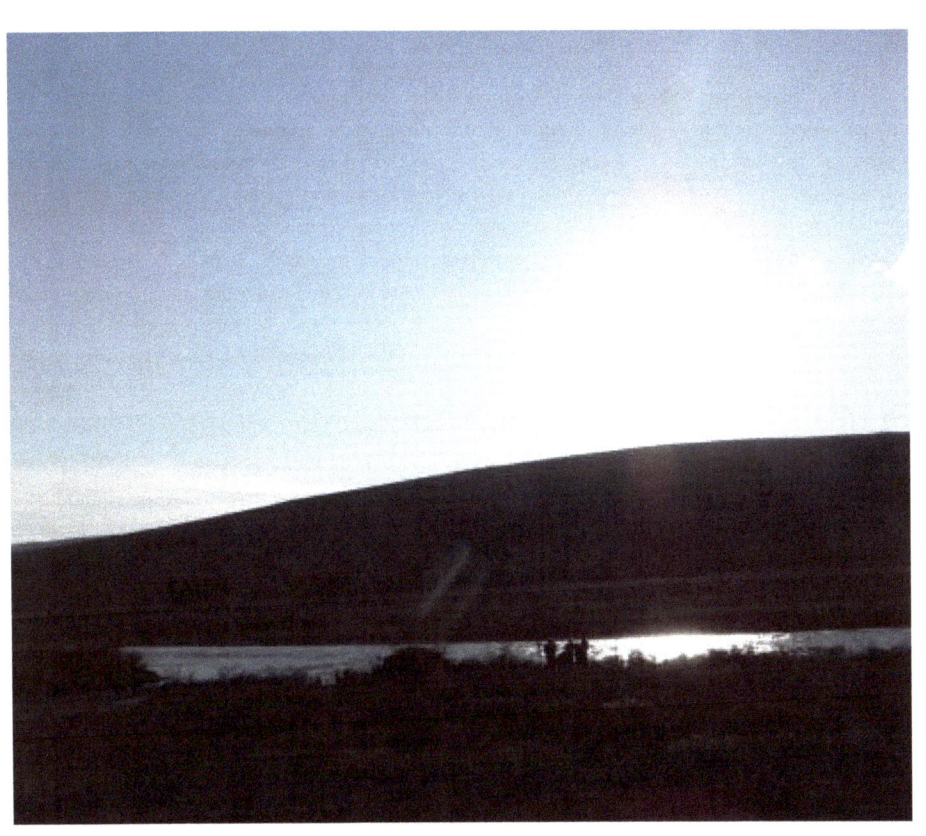

Barbara feeding fish from our dock on Valentine's Pond. As the evening darkens, brim, koi and grass carp come to the dock when we throw out fish food. We spot them with flashlights. We purchased the koi and grass carp in an attempt to control the water lilies and invasive species grass in the pond.

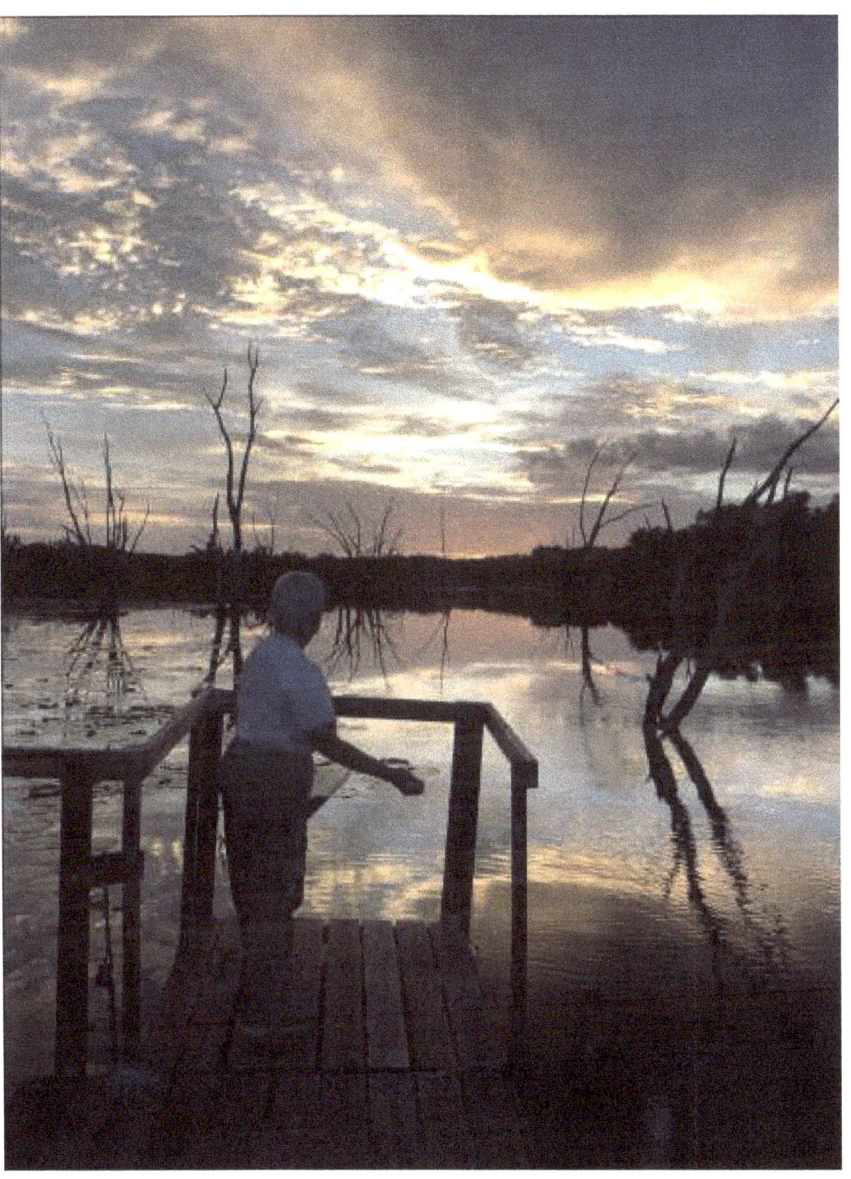

Sunset on the mighty Yukon River between Eagle and Circle, Alaska. Photo from our 160 mile canoe trip in July 2016. Because we were 150 miles south of the Arctic Circle, the sun did set briefly every night. However, the night never became dark enough for us to see the northern lights.

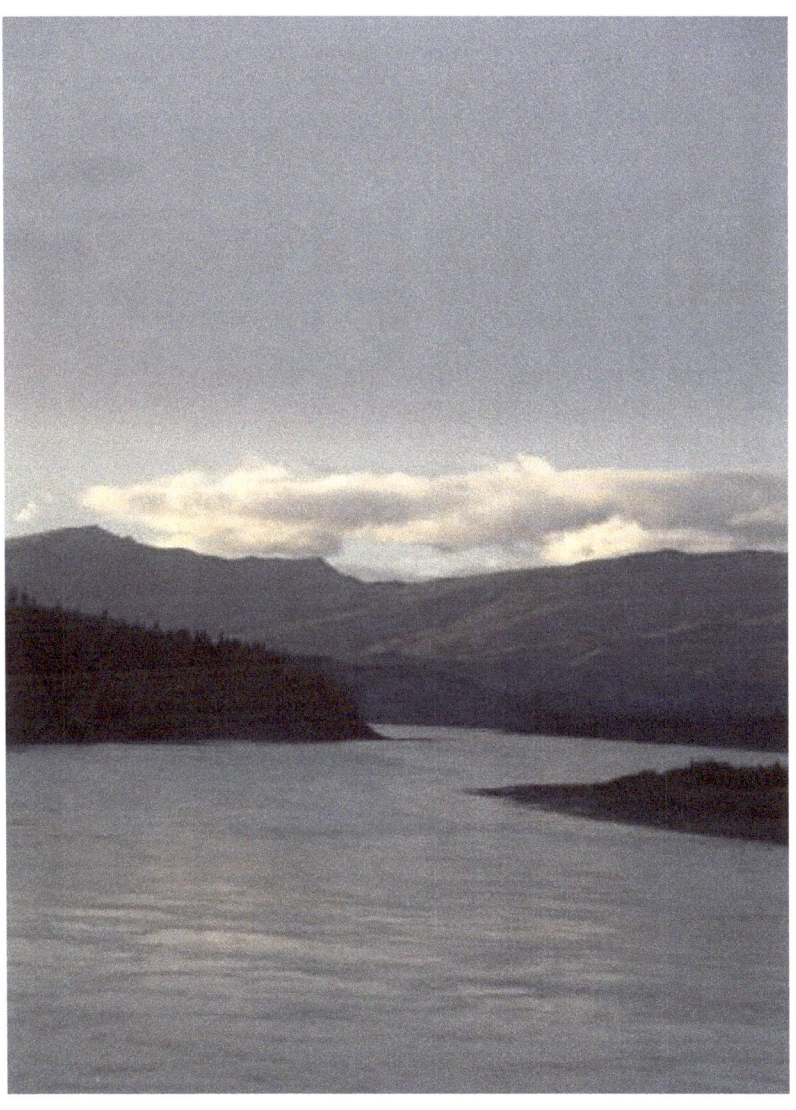

The southern coast of Oregon had some of the most beautiful sunsets we have ever seen. On this evening we sat on a driftwood log eating a pint of vanilla ice cream topped with ripe blackberries we picked from bushes behind our motel.

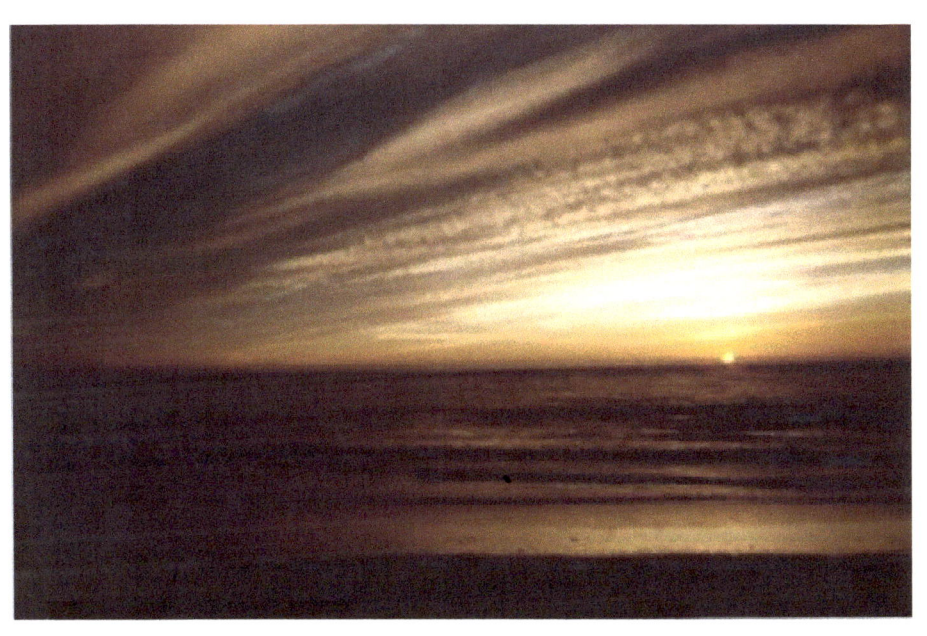

Sunset from our porch in early November, 2018. Live oaks in South Georgia keep their leaves through winter. They shed them in the spring when they are pushed out by new growth. This photo is not color enhanced.

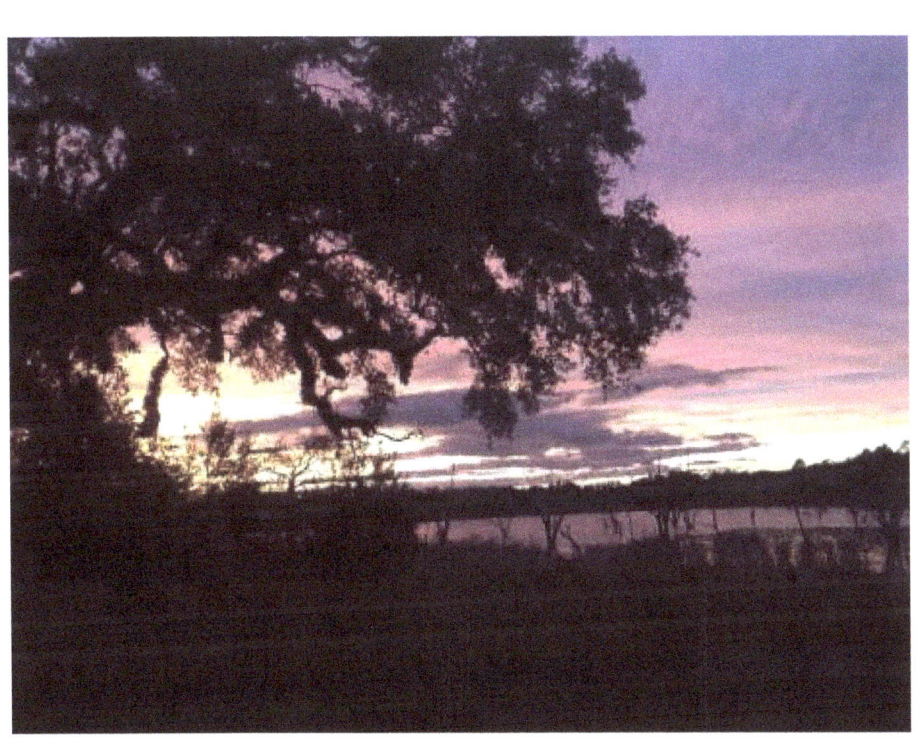

In May 2014 we canoed for four days on the Milk River in Alberta, Canada. It was a twisting prairie river of continuous rapids. On the evening of our second day, I climbed a hill above our camp and photographed the river in the fading light.

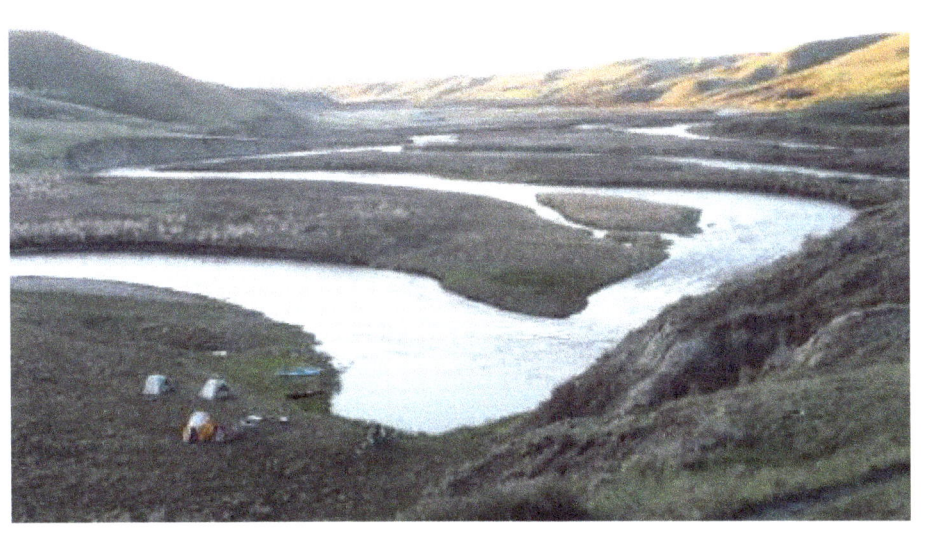

In early September 2008 Barb and I hiked the Brazeau River Trail in Banff National Park, Canada. Our timing couldn't have been worse as we were caught in snow, sleet and raging thunder storms. Here we hurry to the next campground.

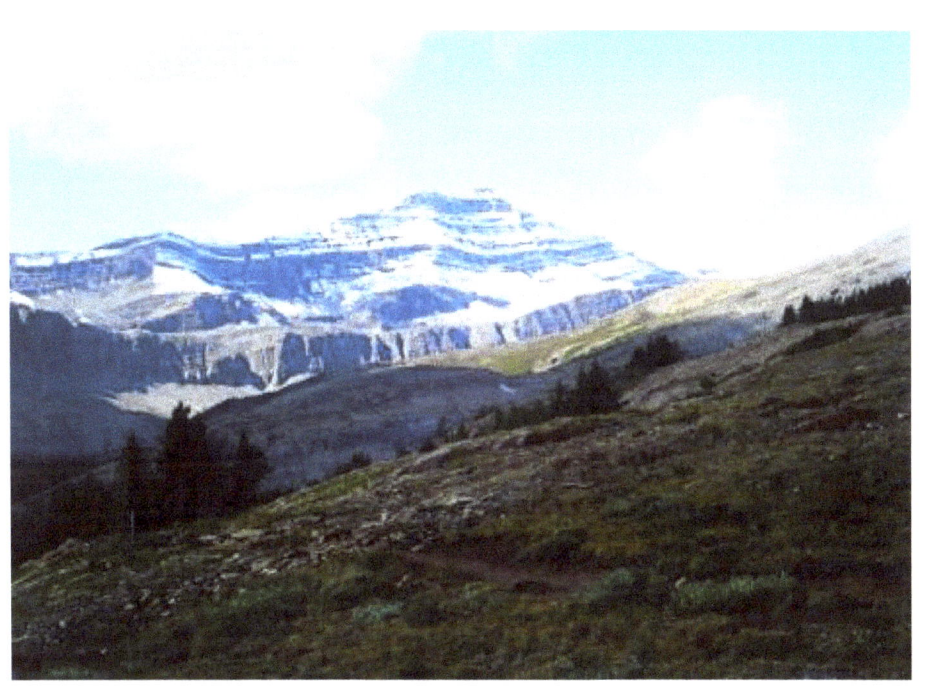

An August afternoon and evening of thunderstorms from our porch in Bainbridge. In late summer moisture rising off the warm water in the Gulf of Mexico creates a parade of rain-dense clouds.

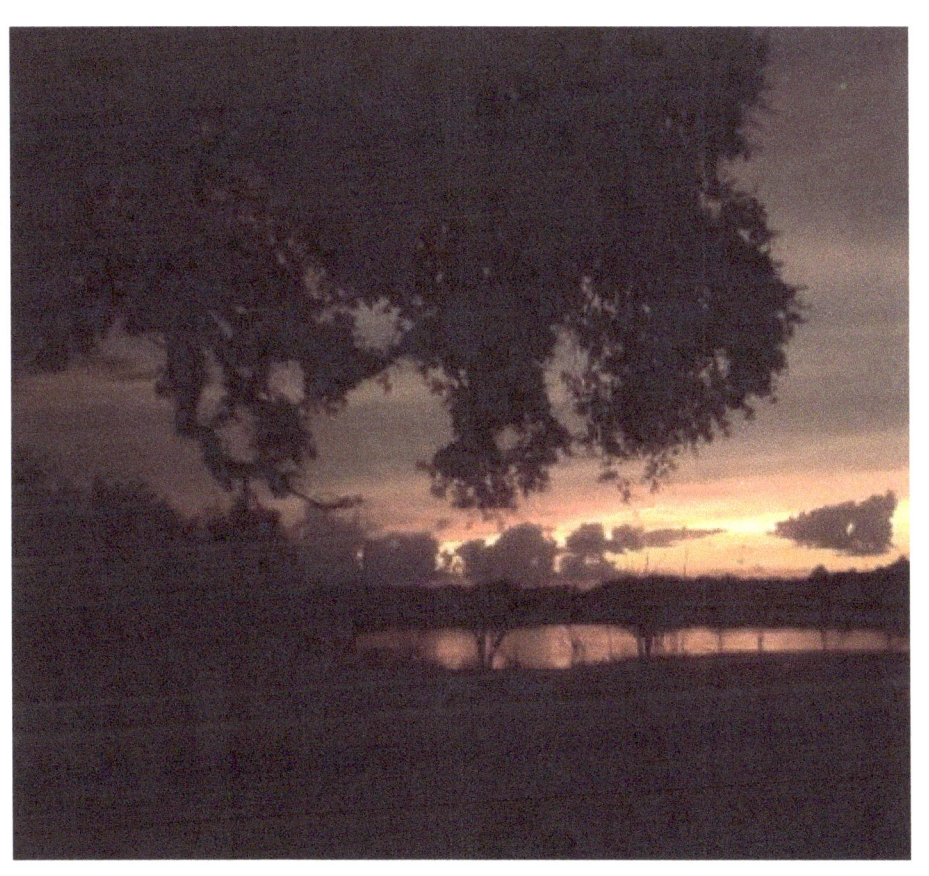

Two canoes above the Arctic Circle on the Kokolik River, June 2022. A quiet evening with a sun that never sets. We canoed nine days in a group of eight people in four canoes. Snow on a distant hillside.

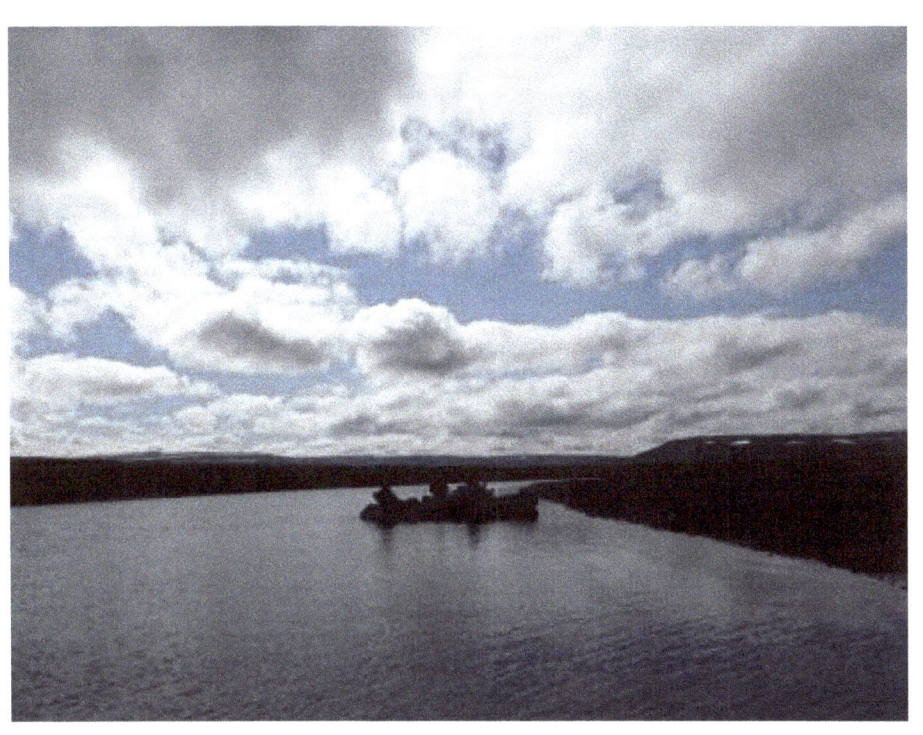

Behind the Coastal Range of mountains on Australia's Northeast Coast lies a dry land of grass, cattle, gum trees and termite mounds. In 2000 we spent a week in this area fossicing for topaz and exploring its strange beauty.

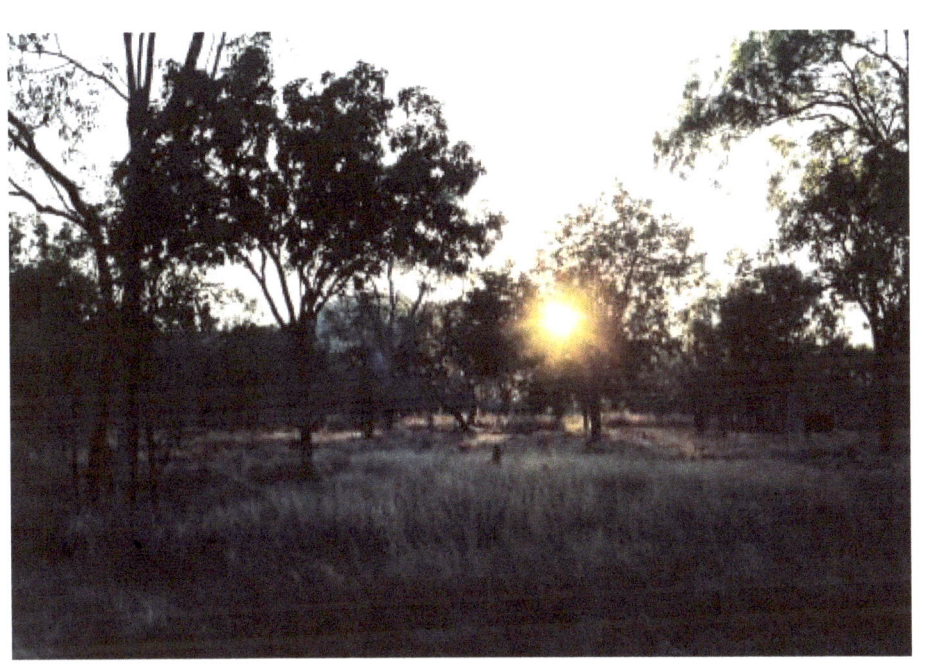

In 1998 Barb and I hiked the trail from
Lanmanulaugar to Porsmark in Central Iceland.
Lonely Planet calls this one of the world's great
hikes. It was certainly the most dramatic we have
undertaken. Cinder deserts, glaciers, steam vents, icy
rivers. The interior of Iceland is uninhabited and
uninhabitable. Along the way are huts where at the
end of the day you can sleep on the floor or in bunk
beds.

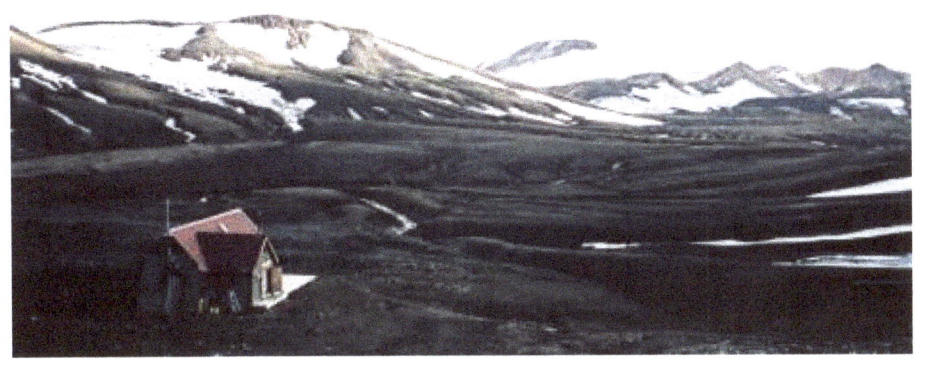

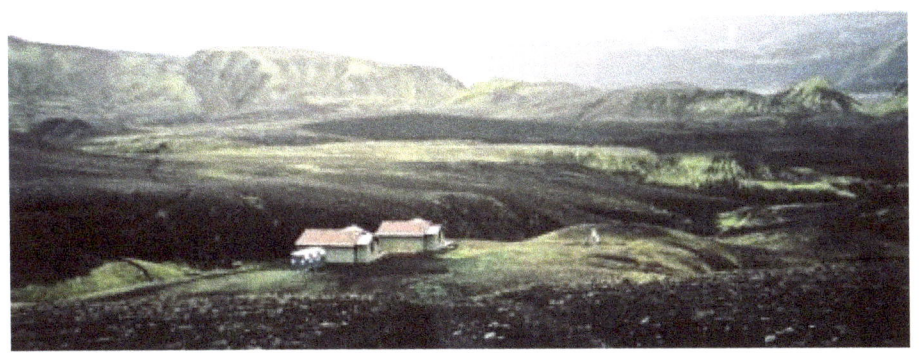

In early June 2006 Barb and I took Matthew Cannon and a friend on a canoe trip on the Little Missouri River in North Dakota as a high school graduation present. The river winds through North Dakota's Badlands and the three units of the Theodore Roosevelt National Park. A double rainbow after an evening storm.

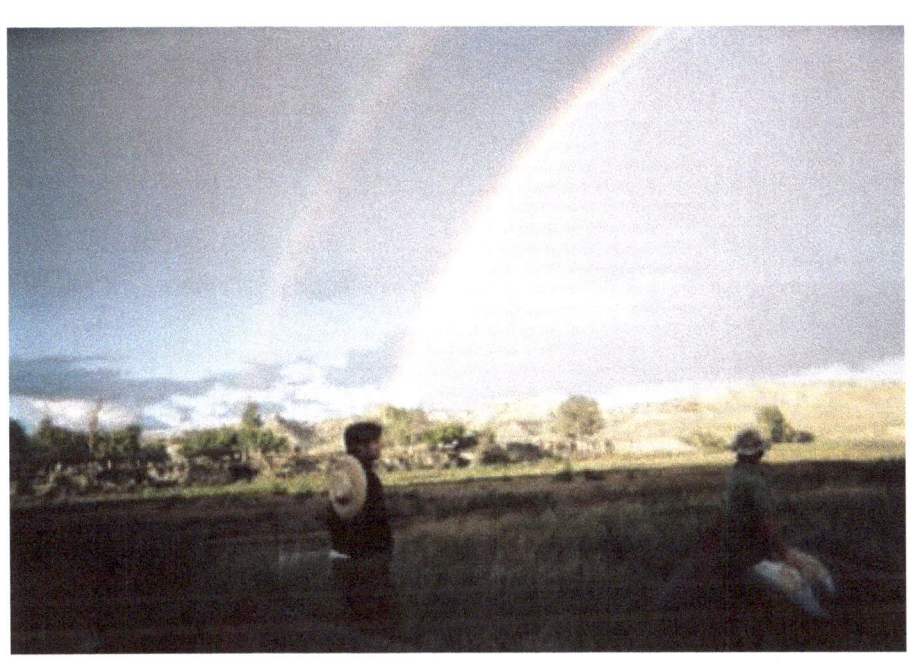

Sunset and a storm on the Noatak River in the Gates of the Arctic National Park above the Arctic Circle in Alaska. This ten day paddle and hiking from Pingo Lake to Matcharak Lake was our first Alaska River trip.

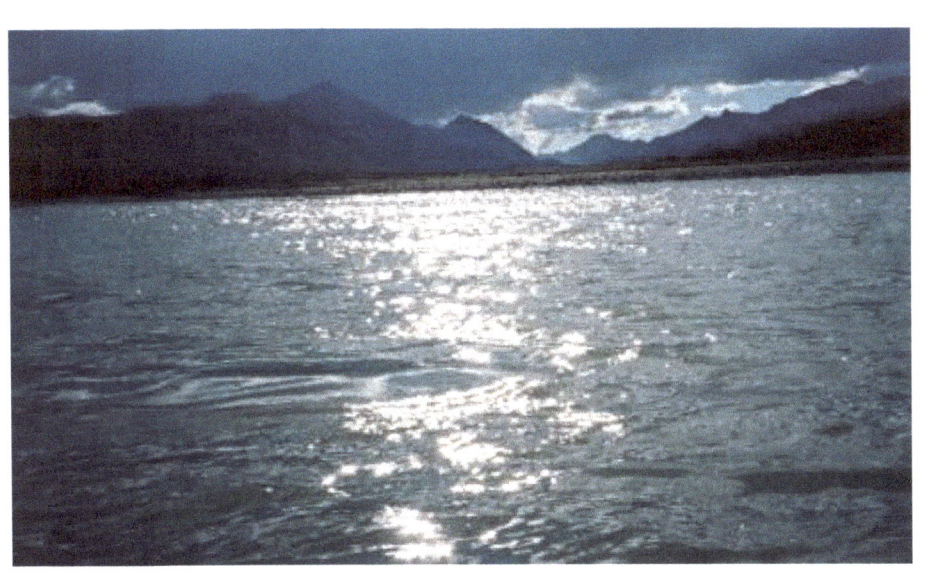

Florence, Italy at sundown. The Arno River and the Cita Vecchia bridge. Florence is a gift to humanity that everyone should experience at least once in their lifetime.

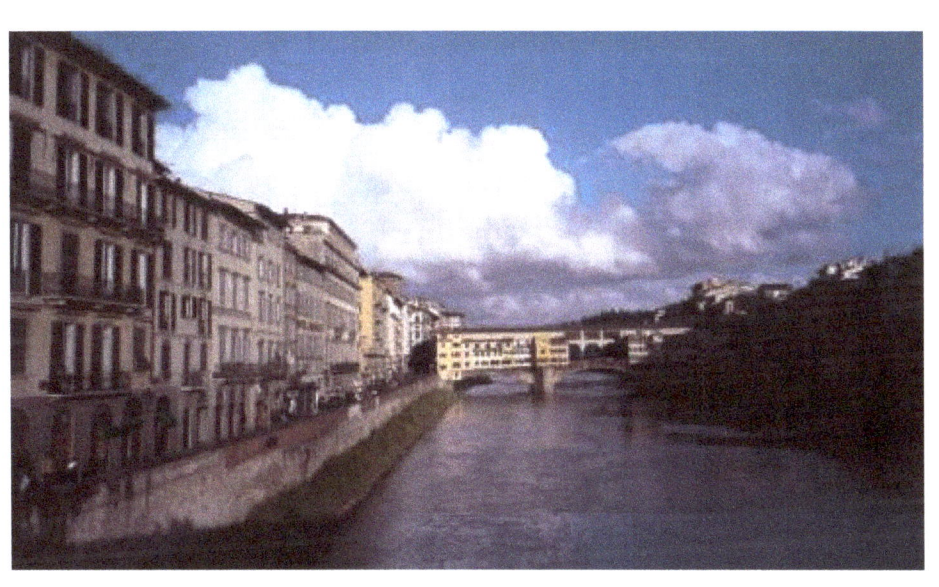

Sunset on our pond from the floating dock that we built with plastic 55 gallon drums that Barb collected from her job at Marriott. The drowned live oaks stretch their branches to the sky. Their wood is so hard one can barely pound in a nail.

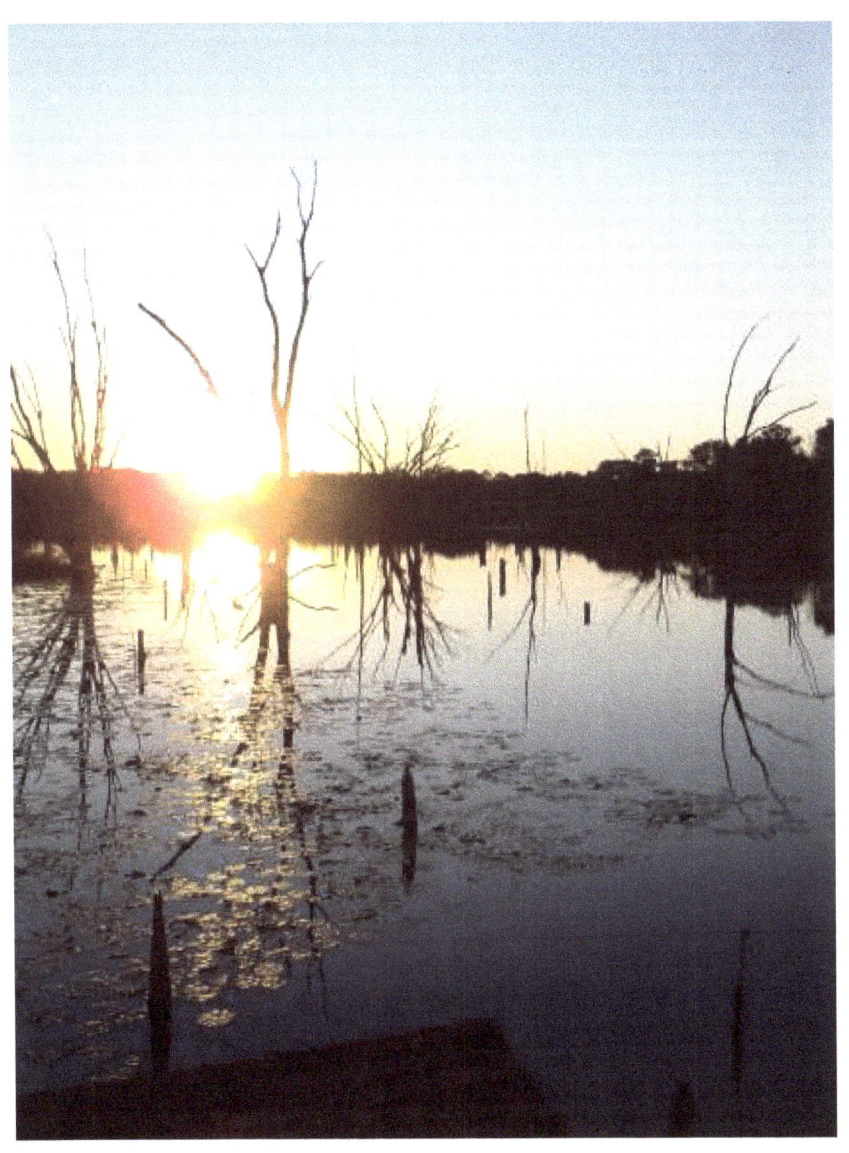

Harvesting peanuts is dirty, dusty business. The sandy soil has to be free of moisture so that the harvested peanuts don't mold. October 2018.

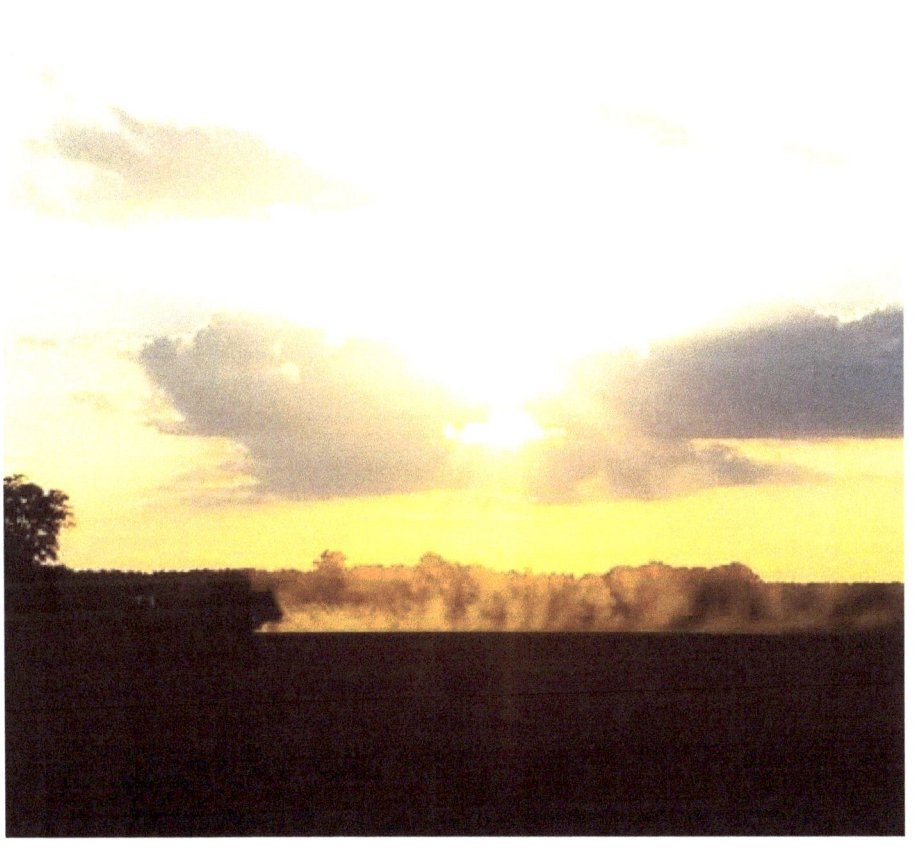

The Missouri Breaks National Wildlife Reserve straddles the Missouri River in Central Montana. This is the route of the Lewis and Clark Expedition in 1804-1806. In this photo we are camping in one of the campgrounds Captain Clark used when he fled from the Blood Indians in 1806.

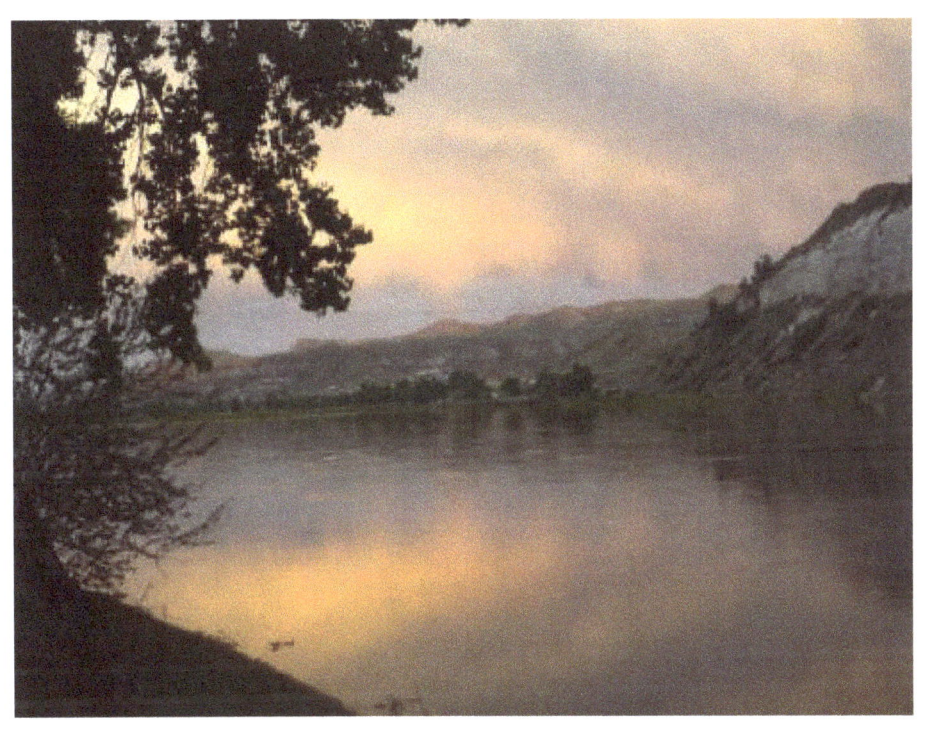

High cirri-cumulus clouds promise a calm night as they float above our pond on a September evening in 2020.

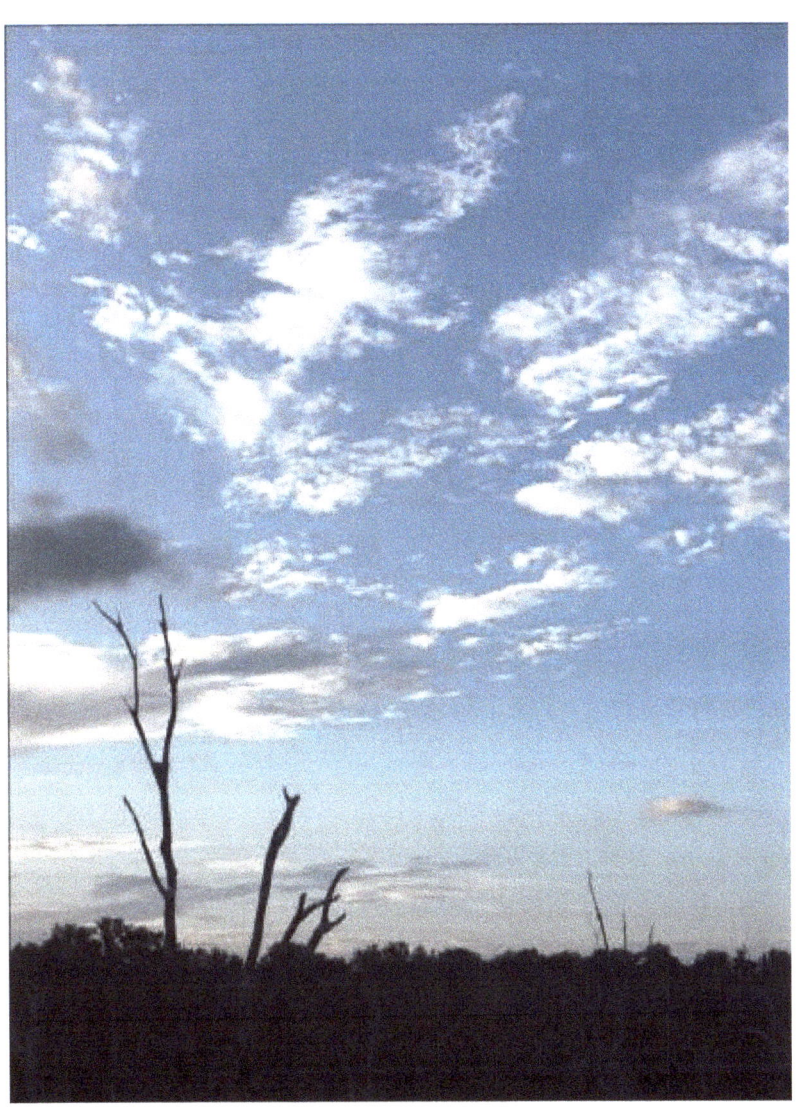

Sunset and storms in the Grand Tetons of Wyoming. In September 2011 we were supposed to hike the Heart Lake Trail in Yellowstone National Park. An unexpected snowstorm cancelled that plan. We hiked around the Tetons instead.

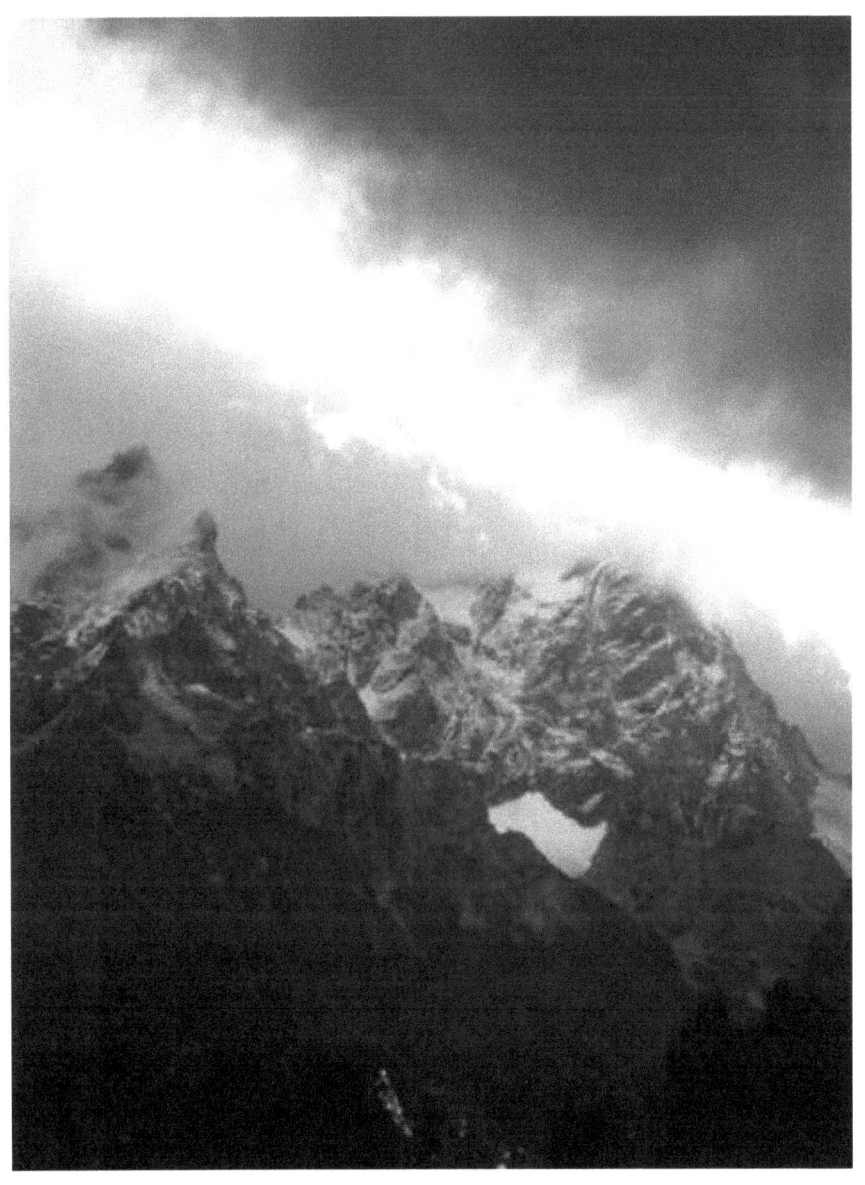

Sunset in Key West, Florida. Barb and I like to drive to the end of a road. In 2014 we drove through Florida all the way to the start of US Route 1. Sorry to say, we found Key West's advertised present a shadow of its fabled past.

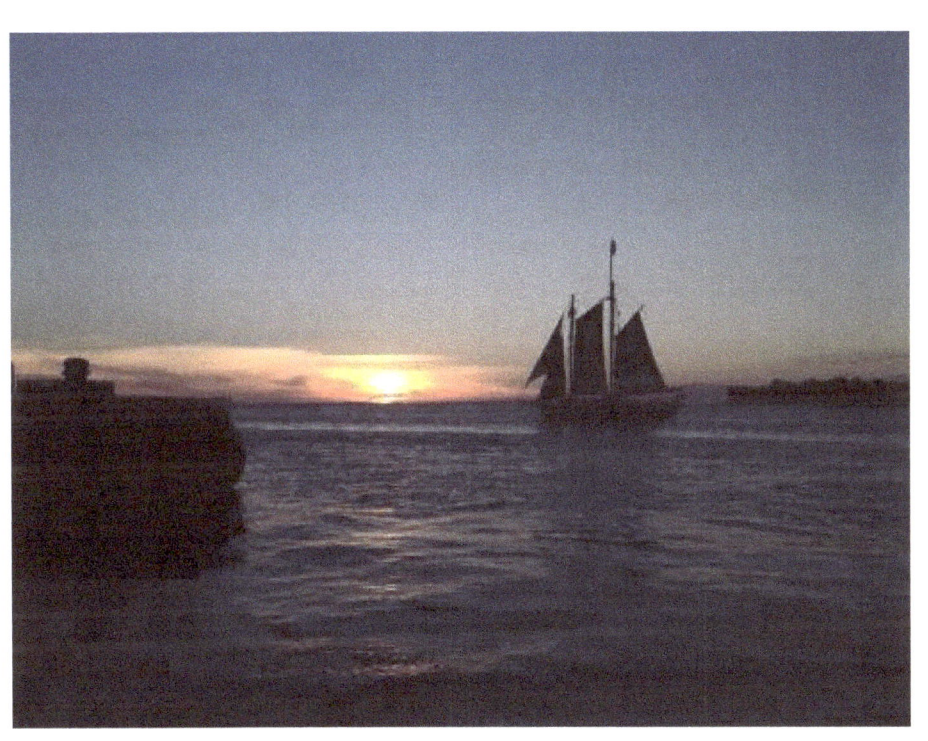

Now and then our pond is as still as a reflective mirror. On those evenings the sunset delivers a double pleasure. September 2019.

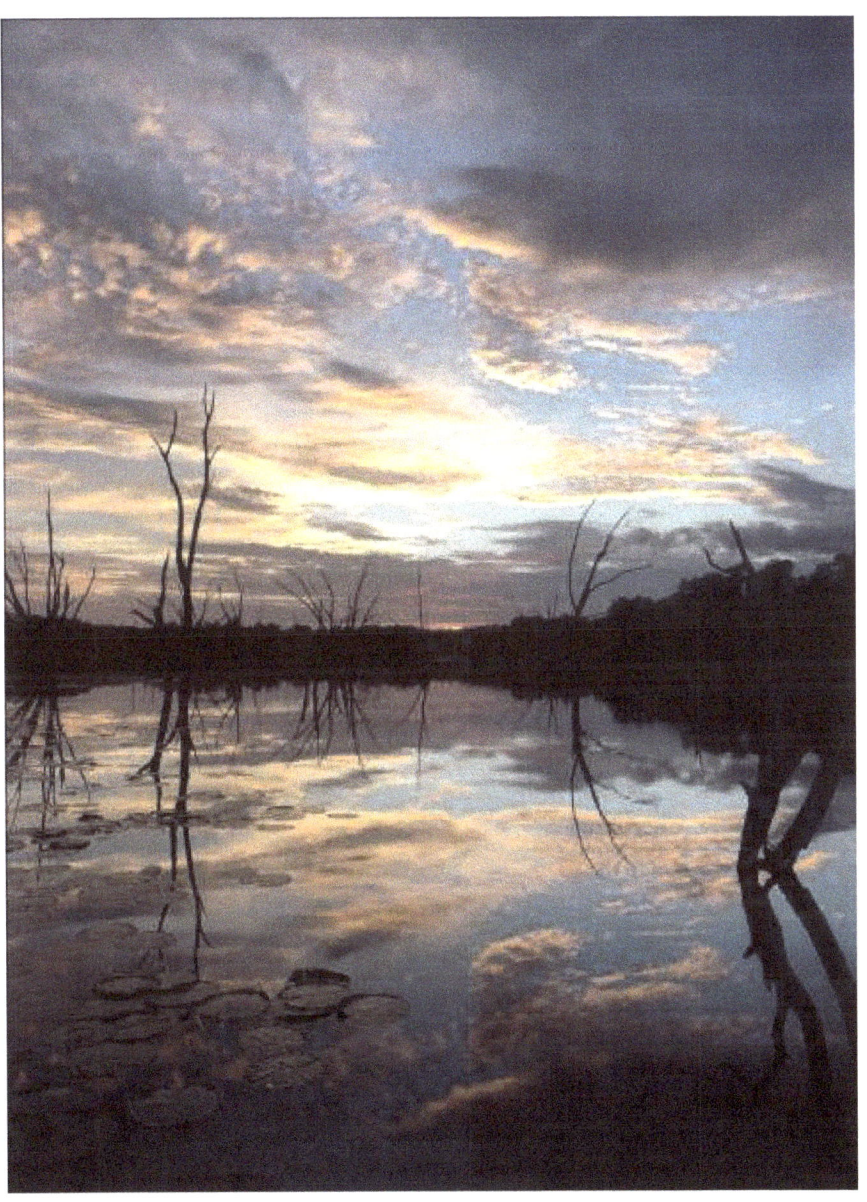

On the hike to Brazeau Lake in Banff National Park in September 2008 we met a group of men who called themselves *The Over The Hill Gang*. They took a special shine to Barb and made sure that we joined them for dinner.

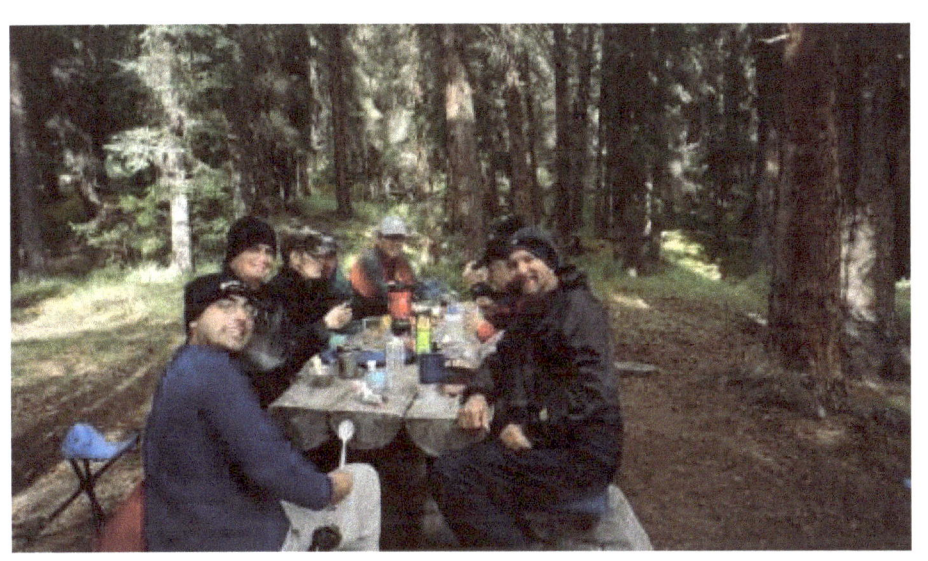

Evening campfire with Ralph and Judy on the Yukon River in July 2016. Anabundance of river drift wood provided us the fuel for a campfire every night. We canoed 160 miles from Eagle to Circle, Alaska in nine days.

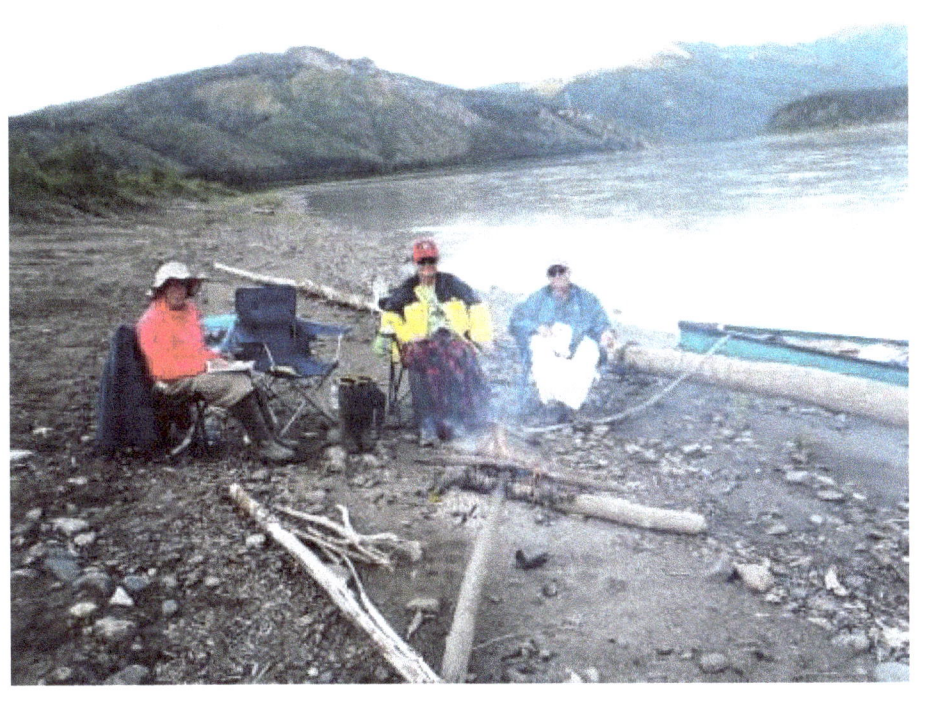

Another sunset in Key West Florida. A lone sailboat with lights sways in the waves.

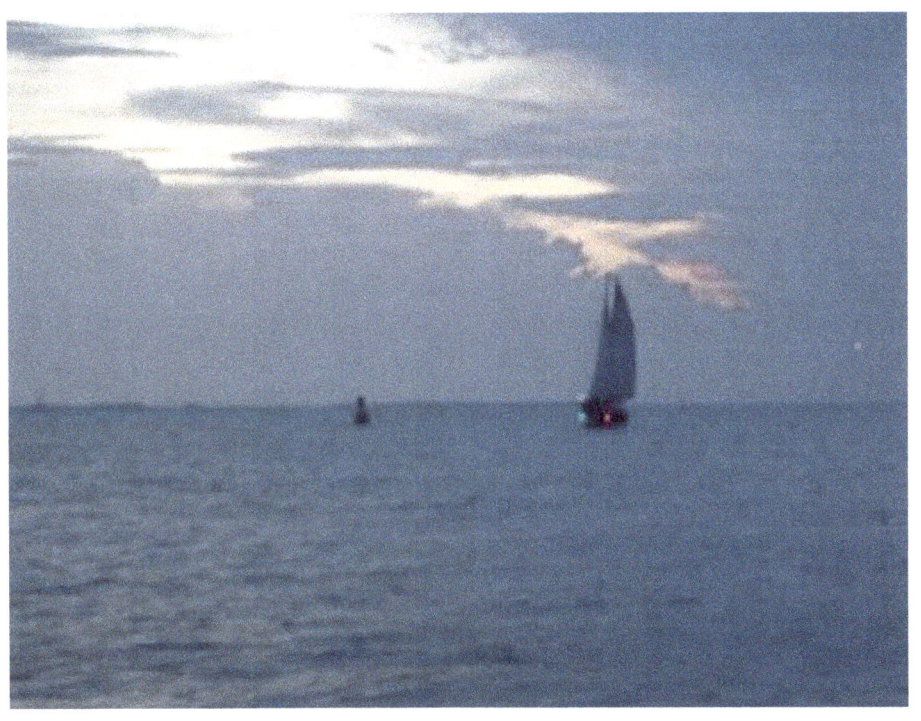

Sunset over our pond in April 2013. The clouds appear to be burning.

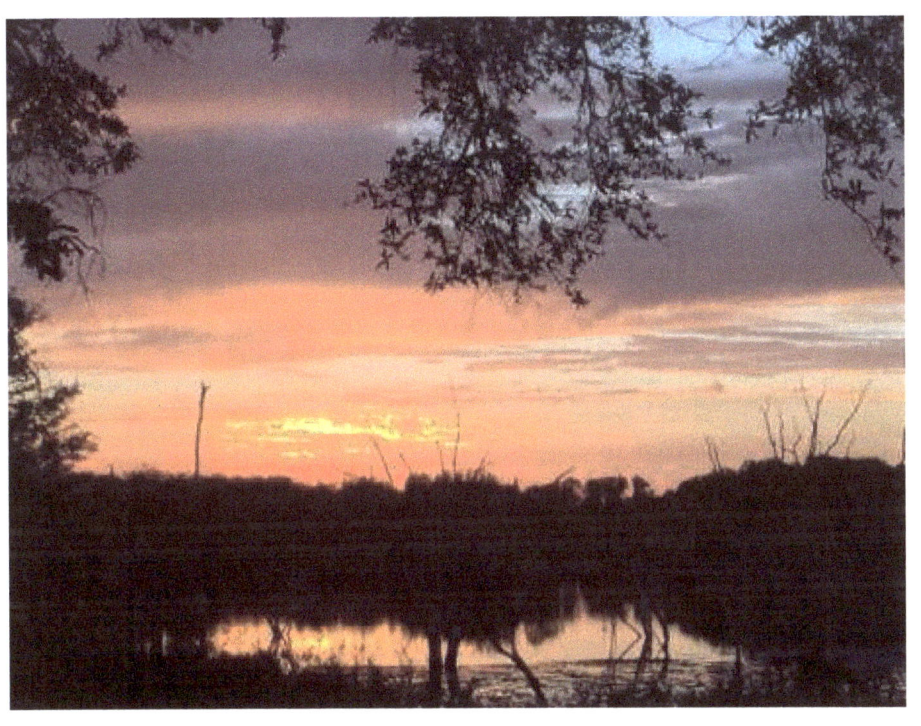

Strange trees on the South Island of New Zealand. In 2015 we took a four day hike on the Kaikora Coast Track staying in farmhand bunk houses. Sad to say the 2020 earthquake destroyed much of this area.

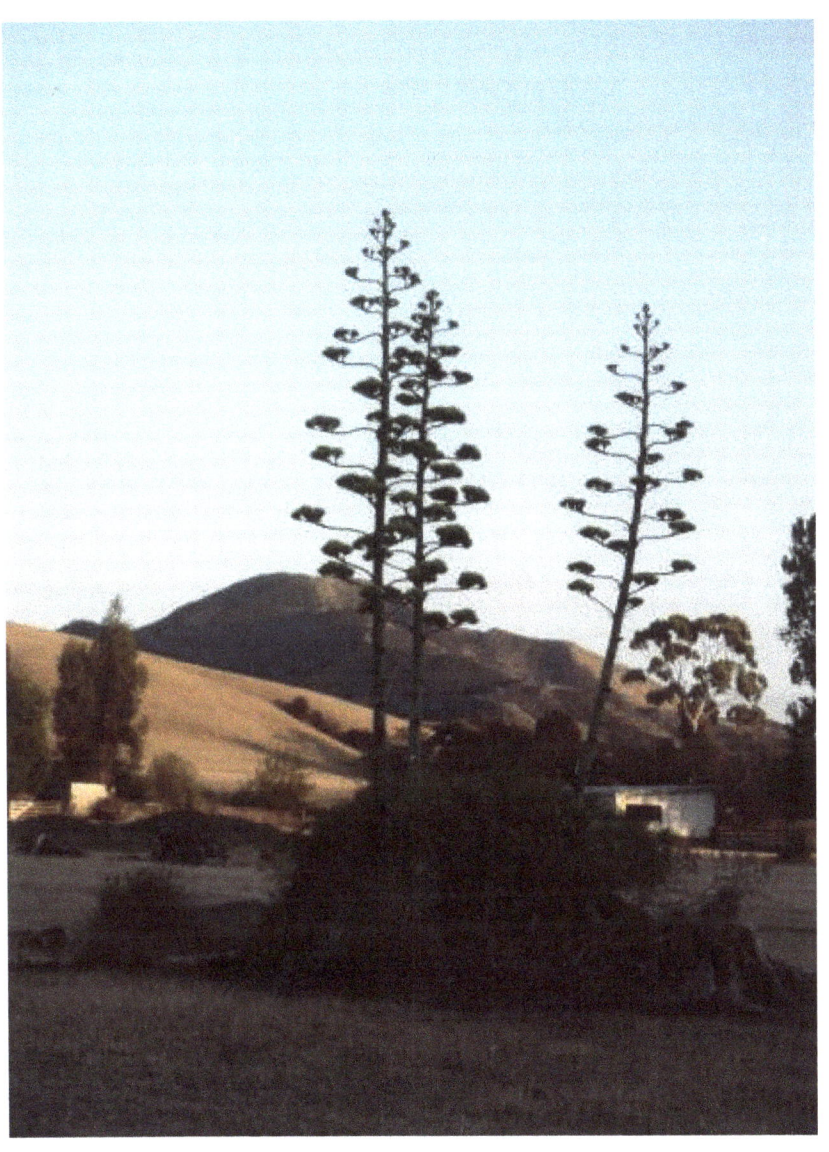

Rainy, foggy night camping in June 2019 on the Yukon River someplace between Dawson, Yukon Territory and Eagle, Alaska. Our canoe seems lonely on the river's edge. As the river rose, we had to pull the canoe further on the shore.

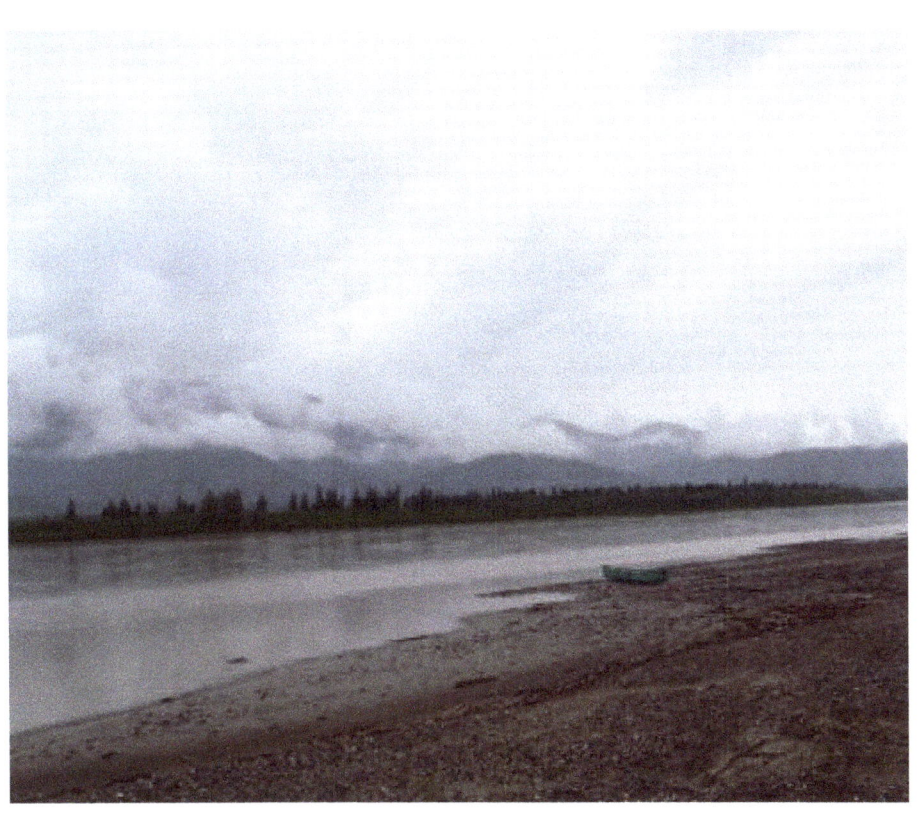

Morris Dancers outside a pub in a small village in the Cotswolds during our ten day walk in June 2017. They dance for various causes. On this evening it was for soldiers injured during the Falklands War. This dancing tradition dates back at least to the Middle Ages.

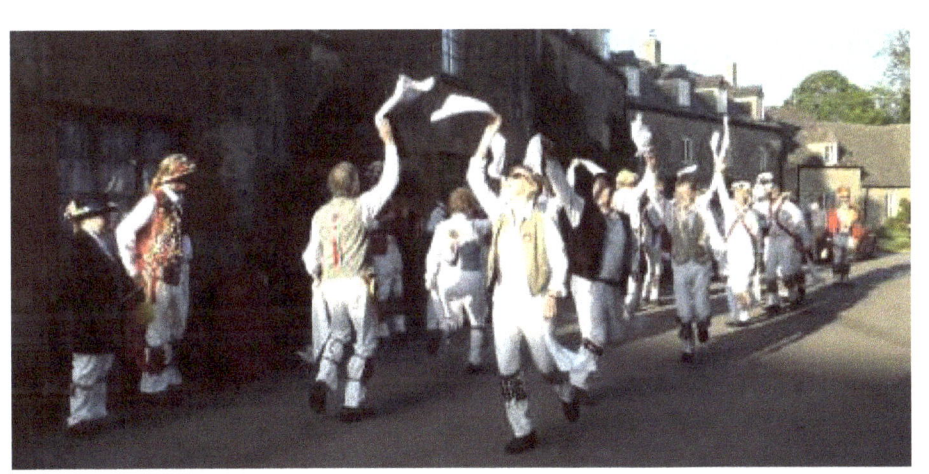

Camping on the Missouri River in Montana at a campsite used by the Lewis and Clark Expedition as they poled and dragged their boats upriver against the stiff current and cold water in June1805. A rainbow wishes us a good evening.

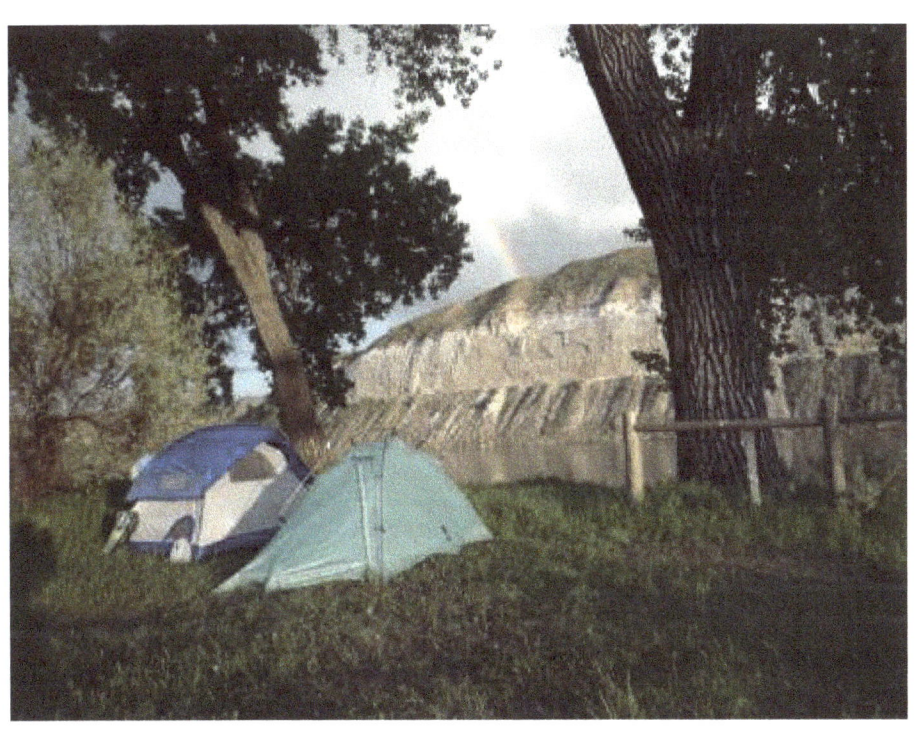

Carrabelle is a sleepy fishing village in the Panhandle of Florida. How it has managed to avoid the so-called development on the Gulf Coast is a pleasant mystery.

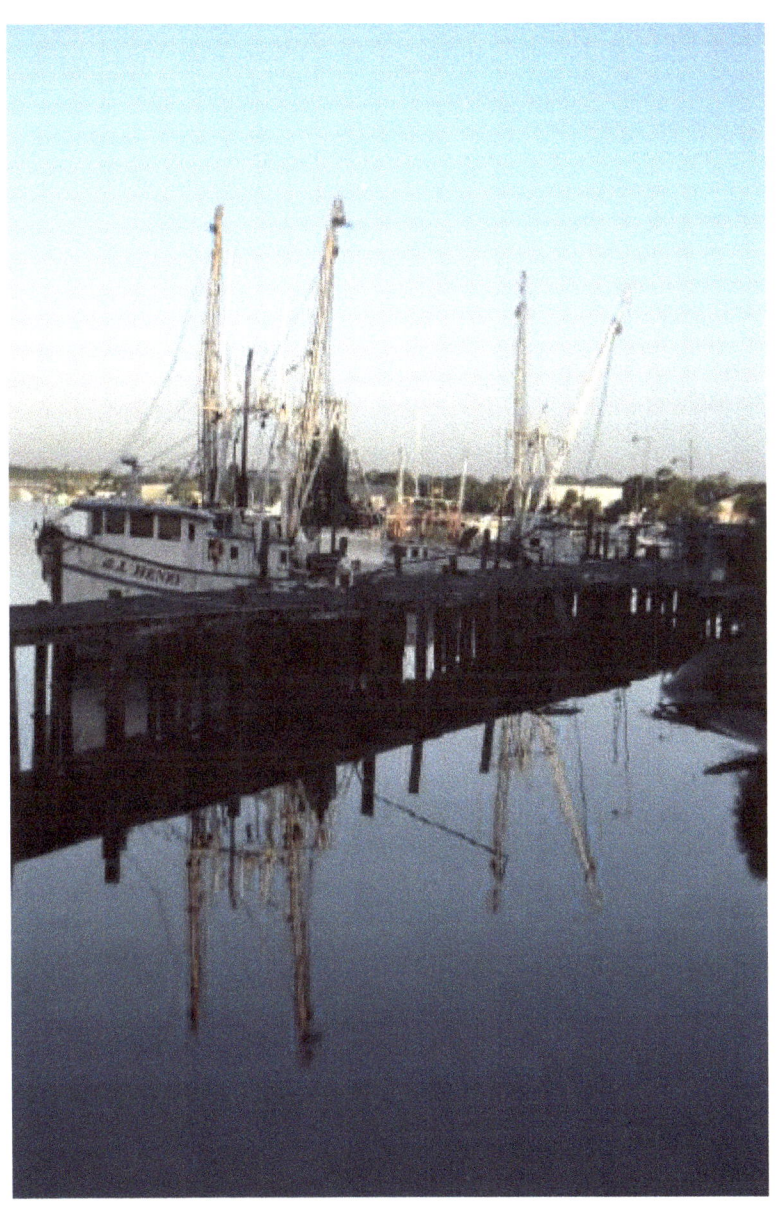

Next to our home in Bainbridge is an old cemetery for members of the Mock family. The graves lie abandoned and untended. The cemetery overgrown. It was nearly wrecked by Hurricane Michael in 2019.

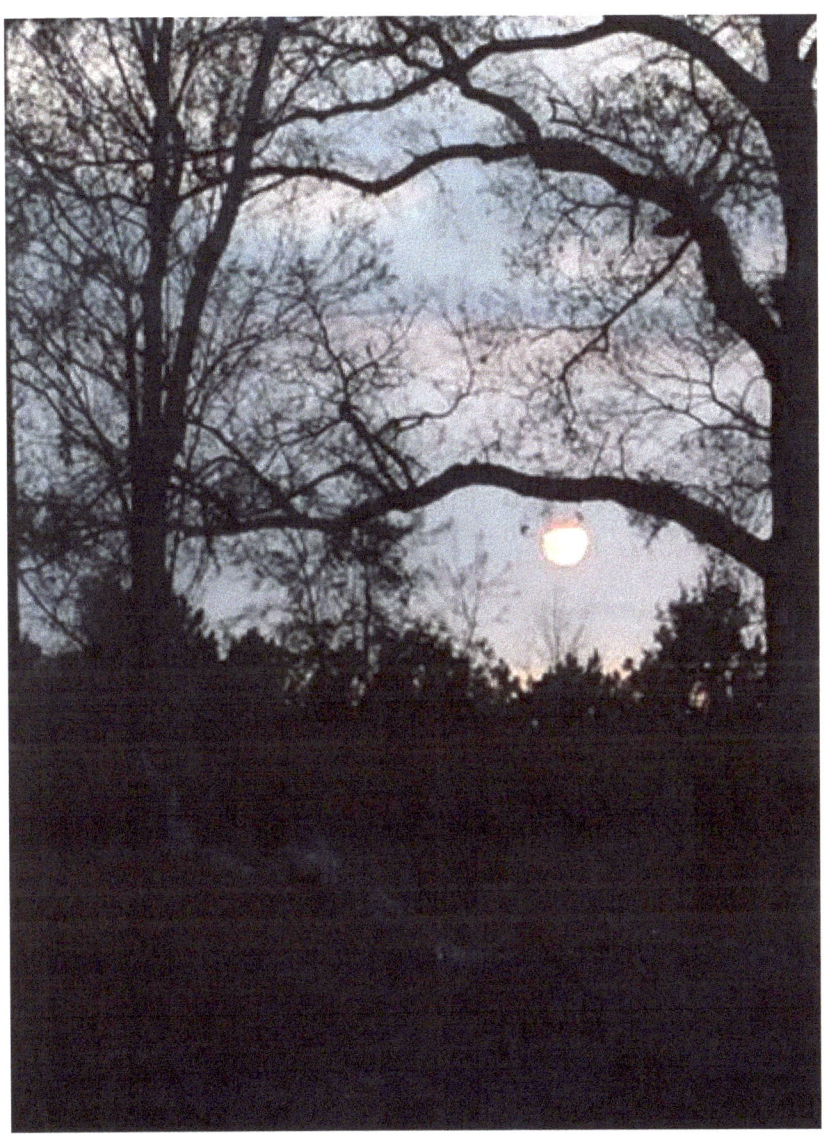

A foggy evening camp on the Yukon River in Alaska in July 2016.

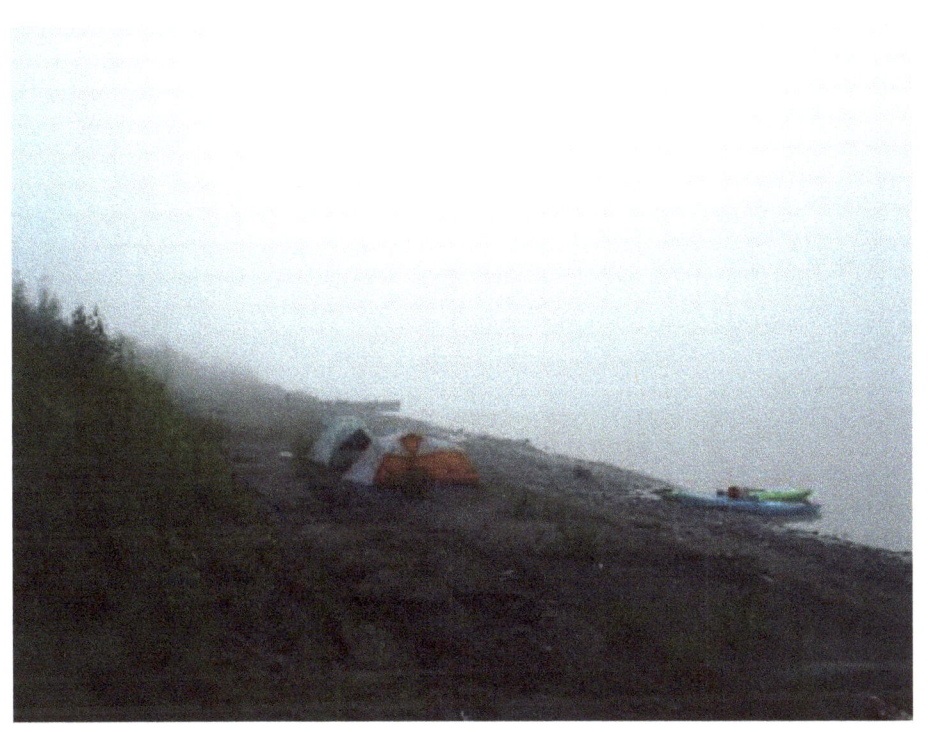

At Christmas time we string bright lights along our porch.
Sunset on a gloomy Christmas Eve is still inviting.

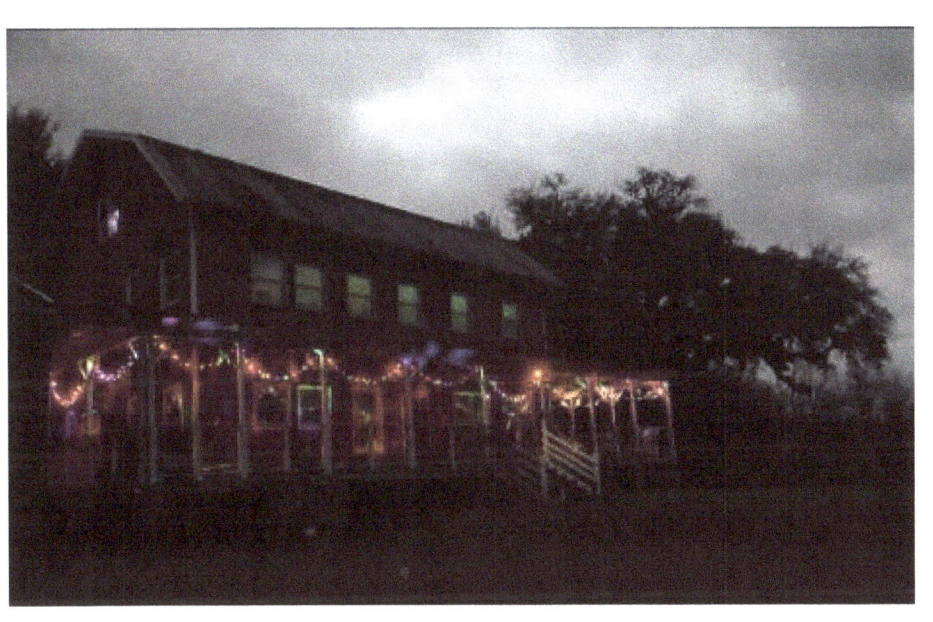

PART 2

MOONSETS

Moonset over our pond with a trailing reflection on the quiet water in June 2018. The moon's brightness overwhelms the camera's electronics as it tries to capture the reflection.

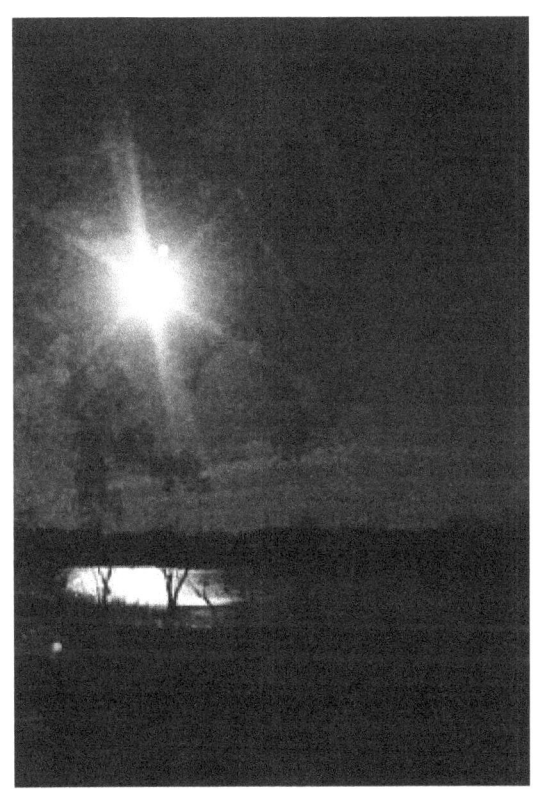

From our porch as the dawn breaks behind me, the moon sets over our pond in late January 2022.

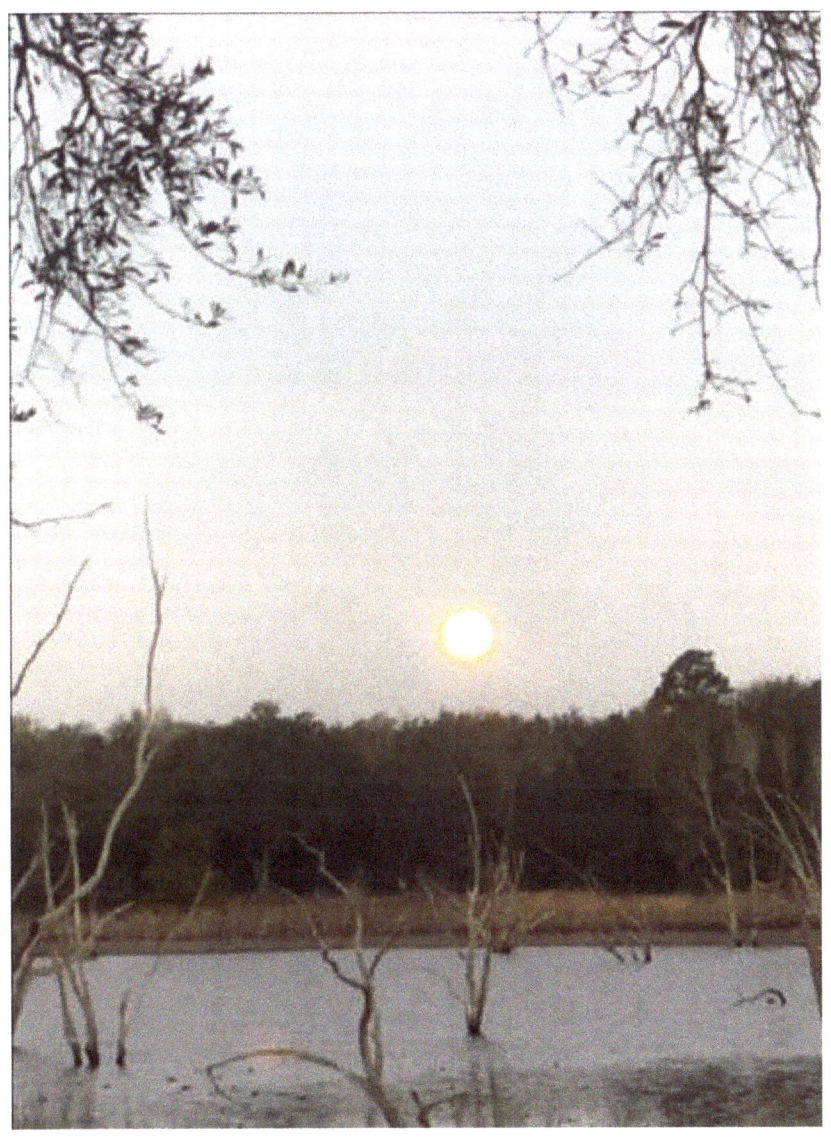

The nearly full moon sets in a cloudy sky outlined by live oaks in April 2020.

On a chilly January morning the full moon falls behind the pond as the dawn breaks. A drowned live oak reaches up to touch his friend.

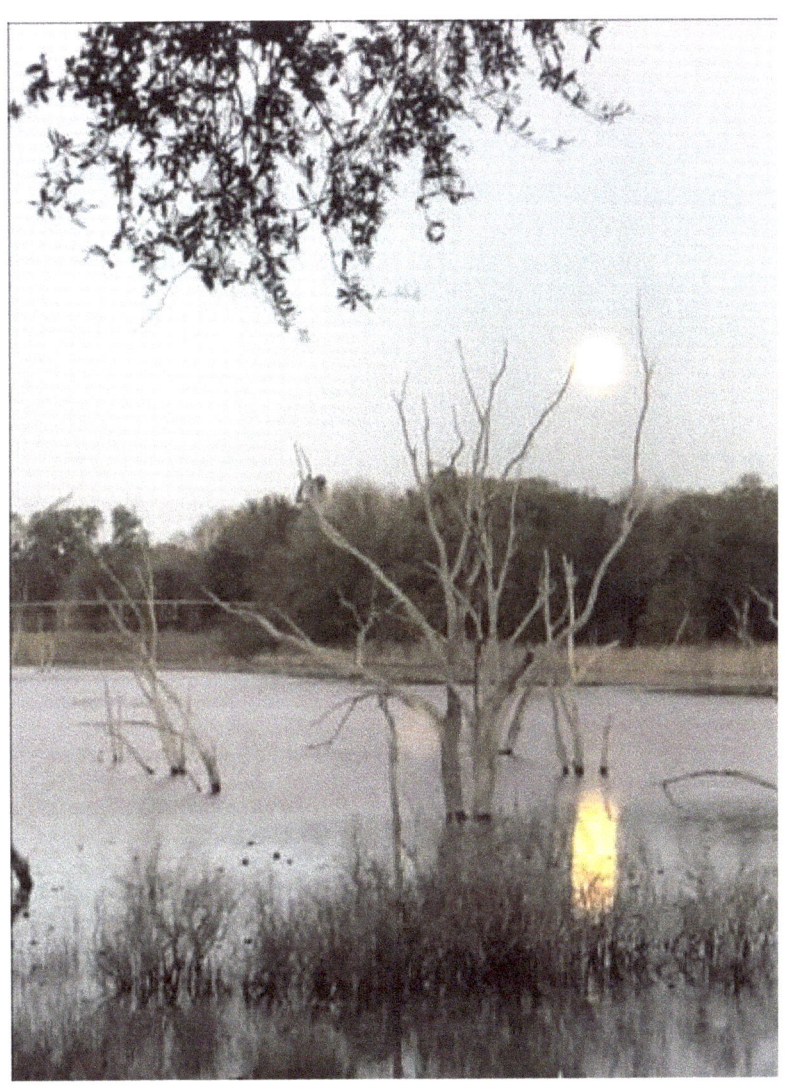

Moonset over a cotton field in December. Some years the cotton can't be picked until late in the season. Here, as the photographer, as the sun rises behind me, as the moon sets in front.

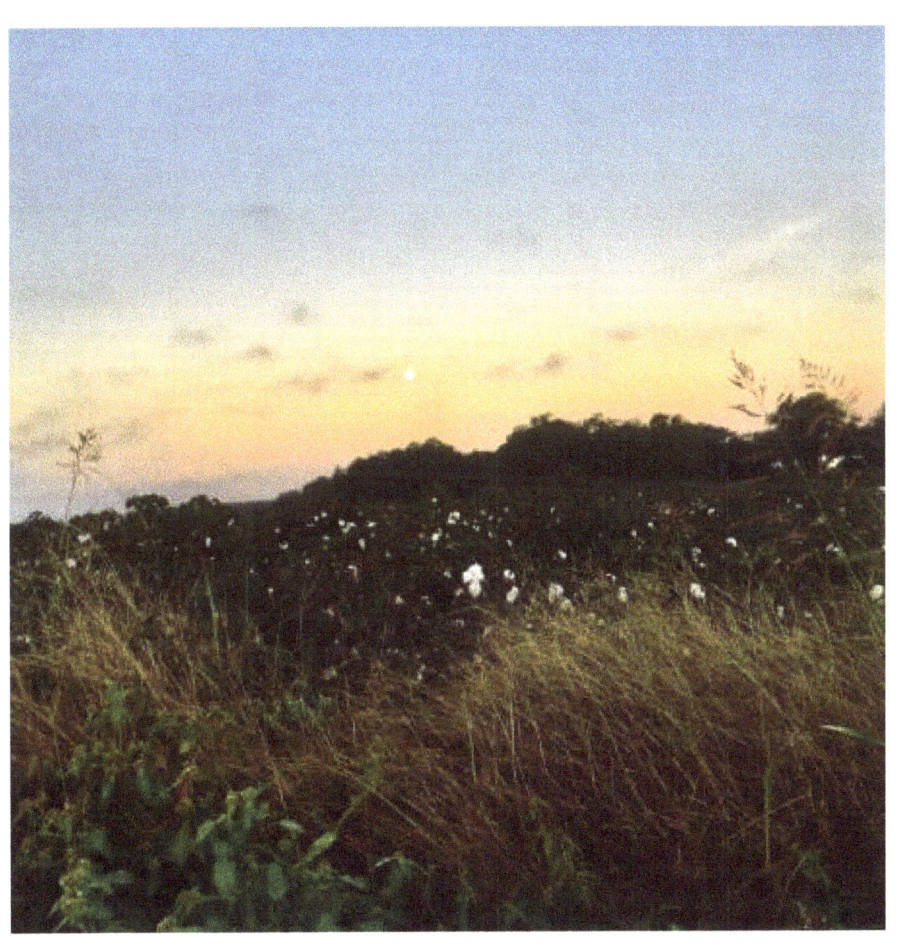

The moon starts its swift descent to drop behind Chief Mountain in Glacier National Park, Montana. September 1997. We were hiking the Belly River Trail in the north section of this beautiful, rugged national park.

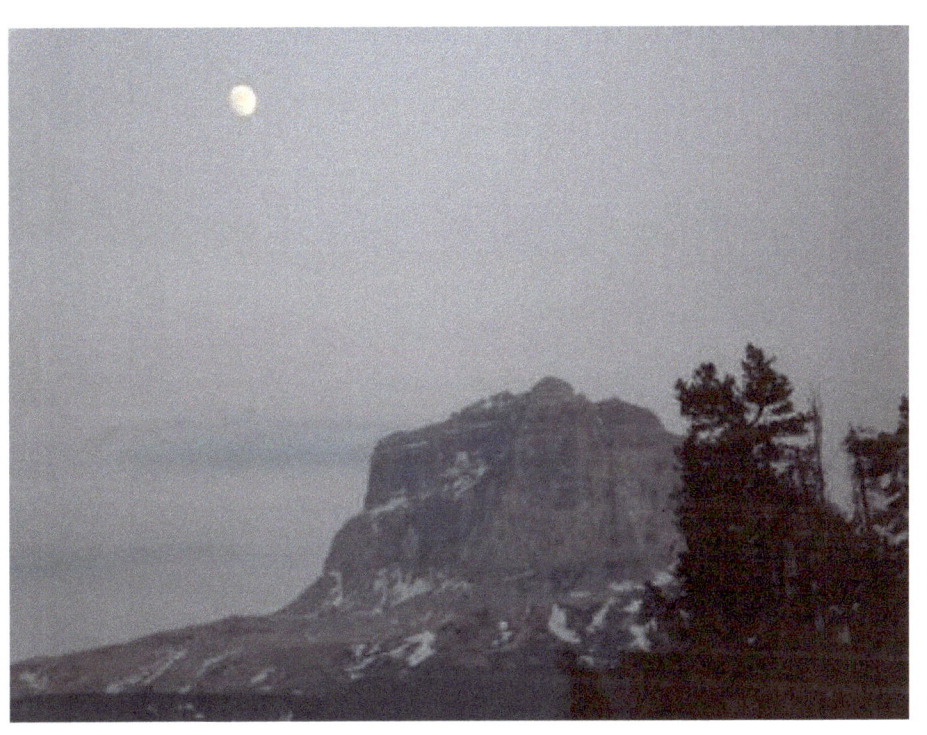

I hope you've enjoyed our photos of sunsets and moonsets. Please visit our website for more photos and stories.

Henryandbarbara.com

Paperback Books by Henry available at lulu.com or at our website www.henryandbarbara.com.

Travel Junkies I, Parts 1 and 2

Travel Junkies 2

Travel Junkies 3

Travel Junkies 4

Travel Junkies 5

Travel Junkies 6

Travel Selections

A Trip to Alaska

160 Miles on the Yukon River

Canoeing Five Rivers in Alaska

Canoeing Six Rivers in Alaska

A Canoe Trip on the Yukon River from Dawson to Eagle (Almost)

A Canoe Trip on the Missouri River with Chip

A Canoe Trip on the North Fork of the Koyukuk River

A Canoe Trip on the Middle Fork of the Koyukuk River

A Canoe Trip on the Kokolik River in Alaska

An Un-cruise Through Alaska's Inner Passage

A Trip to New Zealand

A Walk in Wales on Offa's Dyke Path

A Walk on the South Downs Way in England

A Hike on Hinchinbrook Island, Australia

A Road Trip in Alaska and Yukon 1993

A Hike in Glacier National Park, Montana

A Hike in the White Goat Wilderness of Canada

Young and Single in New York City

Farm Days

The Trigamist

Anello and the Garibaldi Reunion

Anello and the Soldiers of WW II

Poems, Ghost Stories and Palm Readers

The Gloria Cycle: Good Evening Gloria's, Farm Days, and Yvonne

Two One Act Plays (The First Arrow and The Hippie)

Anello – A play

Under the Nurse's Cap

The Weenie Clinic

The I.M.P. Affair (Book and screen play)

The Adventures of Tony and Woof

Further Adventures of Tony and Woof

Tony and Woof at Uncle Henry's Farm

Recipes from Gloria's Restaurant

More Recipes from Gloria's Restaurant

The Making of a Cookbook

Ulysses Elijah – My Story

Oddments

How We Built Our House

Francois and Salvatore – Skits

Francois and Salvatore – Skits 2

Francois and Salvatore – Skits 3

Francois and Salvatore – Skits 4

A Comedy Evening 1 – The Rehearsal

A Comedy Evening 2 – Another Rehearsal

A Comedy Evening 3 – Still Another Rehearsal

A Comedy Evening 4 – The Last Rehearsal

Scrooge – A Comedy Evening

Two Holiday Plays

The Lost Mural of Ellis Island (with Andrew Sabori)

A Travel Photo Album

Travel Photos 2

Sunrises

Books and Plays by Basil Lucas Edited by Henry:

Eden

Not as the Crow Flies

Parade Rest

Royal Mess

Winter, A Boy

The Journal of Pokey Perkins

The Right Place for Love

E-Books by Henry available at amazon.com and lulu.com:

A Walk on the Dingle Way, Ireland

A 100 Mile Walk on the South Downs Way in England

Canoe the Noatak River, Gates of the Arctic NP, Alaska

A Walk through Tuscany, from Florence to Siena, Italy

A Canoe Trip on the Missouri River, 100 Miles in Montana

A Canoe Trip on the Yukon River from Dawson to Eagle

A Canoe trip on the Middle Fork of the Koyukuk River

A Hike in Iceland on the Thorsborne Trail

A Hike in Needles, Canyonlands National Monument, Utah

Hike the Brazeau River Trail, Jasper National Park, Canada

A Hike in the Canadian Rockies, The White Goat Wilderness

A Hike on Hinchinbrook Island, Australia

A Bicycle Trip in Holland, Leiden to Haarlem.

Explore Alaska by Canoe and a Rent-A-Wreck Van

Ghosts, Spirits and Palm Readers.

Anello and the Garibaldi Reunion in Sicily

Anello and the Soldiers Returned From WW II

Exploring, Hiking and Biking in New Zealand

Ulysses Elijah – My Story

A Walk on Offa's Dyke in Wales

Scrooge – A Comedy Rehearsal

Kaikora Coast Track Walk

Otago Central Rail Trail

The Queen Ann's Way

Travel Junkies 1 - Part 1

Travel Junkies 1 - Part 2

Travel Junkies 2

Travel Junkies 3

Travel Junkies 4

Travel Junkies 5

Travel Junkies 6

Canoeing Six Alaska Rivers

New York City Days

The Adventures of Tony and Woof

More Adventures of Tony and Woof

Tony and Woof at Uncle Henry's Farm